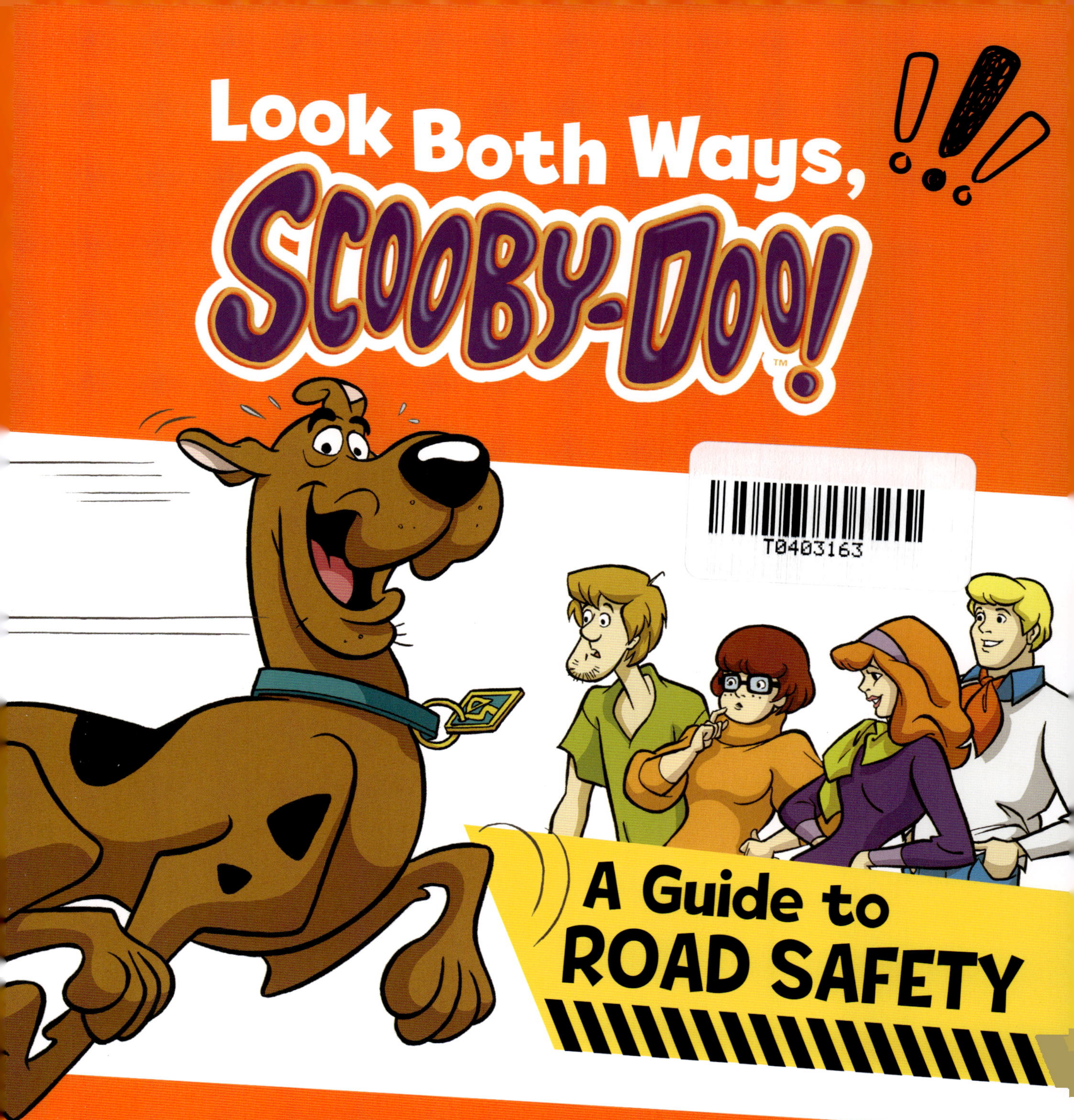

by Steve Korté

PEBBLE
a capstone imprint

Published by Pebble, an imprint of Capstone
1710 Roe Crest Drive, North Mankato, Minnesota 56003
capstonepub.com

Library of Congress Cataloging-in-Publication Data is available
on the Library of Congress website.
ISBN: 9798875220678 (hardcover)
ISBN: 9798875220623 (paperback)
ISBN: 9798875220630 (ebook PDF)

Summary: Scooby-Doo and gang are prepared to teach kids all the rules
of the road and keep them safe.

Image Credits
Capstone: Bobbie Nuytten, 2 (top) and throughout, 12 (top) and throughout;
Getty Images: CasarsaGuru, 18, donald_gruener, 12, Halfpoint Images, 26,
photosaint, 19, praetorianphoto, 22, StockPlanets, 6; Shutterstock: arthierry, 9,
Davor Geber, 10, Idealphotographer, 20, Jayakri, 14, Krakenimages, 17, 28, Makhh,
24, Maria Borodulina, 16, Mirror-Images, 15, Neil Bussey, 27, PeopleImages–Yuri
A, 25, Pincasso, 7, Polina Tomtosova (doodles), 1 and throughout, Prostock-
studio, 4, Rawpixel, 8, Roman Samborskyi, 13, Samuel Borges Photography,
5, Sorapop Udomsri, 21, watercolor 15 (notepad), back cover and throughout,
wavebreakmedia, cover

Editorial Credits
Editor: Christianne Jones; Designer: Bobbie Nuytten; Media Researcher:
Svetlana Zhurkin; Production Specialist: Katy LaVigne

Printed and bound in China. 6274

Keeping Crystal Cove safe from monsters and ghosts is a full-time job for the Mystery Inc. gang. A lot of danger looms outside, especially by roads. Road safety means keeping yourself and others safe when you are on or near a road. When you don't know what to do, just ask Scooby-Doo!

I didn't hear my alarm and am running late for school. I need to cross the street quickly to catch the school bus.

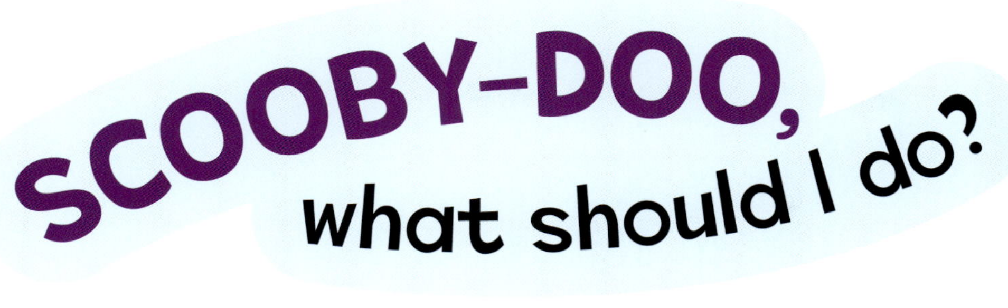
SCOOBY-DOO,
what should I do?

You should stop, look, and listen before you cross the street. Stop on a sidewalk or curb. Look left, right, and then left again to check for vehicles. Listen for vehicle sounds, like an engine or horn.

BEEP!
BEEP!
Knock! Knock!
Who's there?
Cargo.
Cargo who?
Cargo "Beep! Beep!"

We just pulled into the parking lot of my favorite store. My dad is talking on the phone, but I'm ready to go in.

SCOOBY-DOO,
what should I do?

You should stay in the car and wait for your dad. Parking lots are busy, and drivers are distracted. Some are looking for parking spots. Others are backing out to leave. They might not see you.

FRED'S PARKING LOT SAFETY TIPS

- Stop when you get out of the car.
- Pay attention to cars around you.
- Stay with an adult.

DON'T FORGET!

Parking lots aren't play areas. Never run around a parking lot, even if there aren't many cars.

I'm standing at a traffic light, waiting to cross the street. The "DON'T WALK" symbol is on, but there aren't any cars coming.

SCOOBY-DOO,
what should I do?

Always wait until the symbol changes to "WALK." There are different types of traffic signs, so you might see a symbol of a walking person. That means you can cross the road.

Look to the left, right, and then left again to make sure no vehicles are coming.

DON'T FORGET!

Never cross the road if you see a hand symbol, if the sign says "DON'T WALK," or if the walking person symbol is red.

It's a perfect day for a bike ride. I want to ride on the road, but there is a lot of traffic. There isn't a bike lane either.

SCOOBY-DOO,
what should I do?

If you bike on the road, use a bike lane whenever possible. Stop at intersections, use proper hand signals for turns, and stay on the right side of the road.

It's also okay to ride on the sidewalk. Be sure to slow down around people. Ring a bell or say "passing on your left" if you need to go around someone.

DON'T FORGET!

Always wear a helmet and leave your headphones at home. You need to hear traffic while biking.

Velma's Bike Safety Reminders

- Stop and look both ways at intersections.
- Use proper hand signals.
- Be cautious at driveways and alleys.
- Yield to pedestrians.
- Pass on the left.
- Ride with traffic on the right side of the road.

The ice cream shop is on the other side of the street, but the crosswalk is all the way at the corner.

SCOOBY-DOO,
what should I do?

If there is a crosswalk available, you should always use it. You might have to walk a little farther, but it will help you stay safe.

Daphne's Street Safety Tips

- Put your phone away, keep your head up, and watch where you're going.
- Stay on sidewalks whenever possible.
- Don't cross the street between parked cars.
- Never cross at bends or turns in the road.

I'm walking to the park to meet my friend after dinner. I want to wear my new shirt, but it's black. It's not a far walk, but it will be dark soon.

SCOOBY-DOO, what should I do?

Whether you are walking or biking, it is important to be seen. Wearing dark clothes is not a good idea. Wear light-colored clothes or clothes with reflective material later in the day. And be sure to be home before dark.

How was your walk in the hills?
It had its ups and downs.

Scooby-Doo and the gang want you to have a fun—and safe—experience on the road. Staying safe on the road means following a few simple rules.

Stop, look, and listen before crossing the street.

Avoid dark colored clothing at night.

Follow the instructions of traffic signals.

Enter a crosswalk whenever possible to cross a street.

It looks like we've got ourselves a road safety plan, gang!
Great! Let's celebrate with Scooby Snacks!
Yum!
SCOOBY SNACKS

Scooby-Doo's
Road Safety Review

1. What should you try to use to cross the road?

a. a bridge

b. a map

c. a crosswalk

2. If you need to pass someone while biking, what should you say?

a. Out of my way!

b. On your left!

c. Move!

3. When crossing the road, you should stop, look, and . . . ?

a. listen

b. talk

c. roll

4. What color would be best to wear when walking at night?

a. black

b. navy blue

c. white

5. Which side of the road should you bike on?

a. left

b. right

c. either

6. How long should you wait to cross the road at a traffic light?

a. Until the signal says "WALK."

b. No need to wait. Go any time you want.

c. Until the walking person signal turns red.

7. Before you cross the street, which ways should you look?

a. right, left, right

b. right and left

c. left, right, left

8. When can you play in a parking lot?

a. never

b. when it's empty

c. when it's full

ANSWERS: 1. c 2. b 3. a 4. c 5. b 6. a, 7. c 8. a

How many signs can YOU find?

There are different warning signs throughout this book. See how many of each you can find!

About the Author

Steve Korté is the author of more than 100 books, featuring characters as diverse as Batman, Bigfoot, and the Loch Ness Monster. As a former editor at DC Comics, he worked on hundreds of titles, including *75 Years of DC Comics*, *Wonder Woman: The Complete History*, and *Jack Cole and Plastic Man*. He lives in New York City with his husband Bill.